DIVIDEND INVESTING
MADE EASY 2022

Imagine how your life would change, if you knew that you were on the proven path to wealth.

CONTENTS

DISCLAIMER

Neither Little Cash Machines LLC, nor any of its directors, officers, shareholders, personnel, representatives, agents, or independent contractors (collectively, the "Operator Parties") are licensed financial advisers, registered investment advisers, or registered broker-dealers. None of the Operator Parties are providing investment, financial, legal, or tax advice, and nothing in this book or at www.Trader.University (henceforth, "the Site") should be construed as such by you. This book and the Site should be used as educational tools only and are not replacements for professional investment advice. The full disclaimer can be found at the end of this book.

LITTLE CASH MACHINES

Dividend stocks are "little cash machines."

Buy one, and stick it in the corner of your living room.

Every three months, it will burp out a nice slug of cash.

If you save this cash, you will soon be able to buy a few more little cash machines.

Pretty soon, they will be all over your house, spraying cash all over your carpet.

And they will keep doing this-- whether or not you get out of bed in the morning.

That's the beauty of dividend investing.

It's simple.

It's powerful.

And it's one of the best proven ways to build wealth.

Ronald Read spent the first half of his life as a gas station attendant.

And then the rest of his life as a janitor at his local J.C. Penney department store.

When he died at the age of 92, he left behind an $8 million fortune.

All of it in dividend-paying stocks.

Well-known stocks like Wells Fargo, Procter & Gamble, Colgate-Palmolive, American Express, and many more.

If you assume an average 3% dividend yield across his portfolio, he was collecting $20,000 every month in dividends at the time of his death.

At the same time that he was probably making just $13/hour as a janitor.

It's a good reminder that you don't need to collect a massive paycheck to become a millionaire.

You just need to spend less than you earn.

And then invest the rest in dividend stocks.

If you invested just $6,300 every year for 50 years, you'd end up with $8 million like Ronald Read.

It's something that anyone can do.

In this book, I'll teach you how.

You are going to learn:

- Exactly how to set up your own portfolio of dividend stocks
- Where to set up a brokerage account
- Which dividend stocks to pick, and which to avoid
- How to super-charge your returns
- How to ride out a bear market
- And much much more

I'm going to help you start your own collection of "little cash machines."

There's no better feeling than waking up in the morning, and suddenly finding that some more cash has been deposited into your bank account while you were sleeping.

As the years pass by, that cash will continue to pile up.

You'll be able to use it to travel the world.

To pay for your grandchildren's college.

To create a secure retirement income.

Or even to buy more dividend stocks.

The choice is yours.

Once you get started, you'll be hooked.

Your life will never be the same, once you see how you can create crisis-proof, inflation-proof income streams in the stock market.

So let's get started.

THE MAGIC OF DIVIDENDS

W e'll begin at the very beginning.

What is a dividend?

To answer this question, we'll need to remind ourselves what stocks actually are.

Yes, it's fun to trade stocks.

But when we trade stocks, we might forget that each share of stock is actually a piece of ownership in a real business.

When you buy a share of stock, you become a partial owner of the business.

And as a partial owner, you are entitled to a share of the profits that the business generates.

Most mature companies will do 2 things with their profits:

1. They will reinvest some of their profits back into the business in order to grow it.
2. They will return some of their profits to the owners.

Profits that are returned to the owners are called dividends.

If you own a dividend-paying stock, you will usually get paid a dividend every 3 months.

This dividend payment will show up as a cash deposit into your brokerage account.

This cash is yours to keep.

There's even more good news:

You probably won't have to pay much in the way of taxes on this dividend income.

If you own the stock in a retirement account (like an IRA), you won't have to pay taxes on dividends until after you retire and start to withdraw the money.

If you own the stock in a regular brokerage account, you probably won't pay any taxes on dividends until your annual income exceeds $77,201.

You can read more about how dividends are currently taxed here:

https://www.corporatemonkeycpa.com/2018/02/22/taxes-on-dividends-and-capital-gains-under-the-tax-cuts-jobs-act/

I'm not a tax professional, so be sure to consult one for your personal financial situation.

Even when your annual income is higher than $77,201, you'll never pay more than 15% to 23.80% taxes on your dividend income.

When you earn money from a paycheck, you could get taxed up to 37%.

But even if you are a billionaire like Warren Buffett, you'll never pay more than 23.80% on your dividend income.

That's one of the perks of being an investor.

It's another reason why it's always better to have your money work for you.

Rather than you working for money.

Think of each dollar that you invest in dividend stocks as being like a little employee that goes out and works for you every day.

Now it's time to talk about "dividend yield."

If you buy one share of The Coca-Cola Company (KO) today, you'll pay

41.55.

This year, Coke is expected to pay these dividends:

- $0.39 on July 2, 2018
- $0.39 in early October 2018
- $0.78 in early December 2018

You can see the last dividend payment is actually two payments in one ($0.39 times 2).

You can read about these things by going to the Coke website and clicking on "Investors," which will take you here:

https://www.coca-colacompany.com/press-center/press-releases/board-of-directors-of-the-coca-cola-company-declares-quarterly-dividend-apr2018

If you add up all of these payments, you will get $1.56.

So if you own one share of Coke today, the company will pay you $1.56 in dividends this year.

If you own 1,000 shares of Coke, you will get paid $1,560 in 2018.

Here's how to calculate the dividend yield of a stock:

Take the annual dividend payment ($1.56 in this case) and divide it by the current price of the stock ($41.55).

In this case, that gives you 0.03754513, or 3.75%.

3.75% is Coke's current dividend yield.

It's a handy way to think about a stock, since it allows you to compare the stock to other asset classes.

Right now the U.S. 10-year Treasury is paying about 3.00%.

And some savings accounts are paying 1.70%.

Savings accounts are essentially risk-free for amounts up to $250,000 (in the U.S. they are covered by FDIC insurance).

The 10-year Treasury is also essentially risk-free, but it can move around a lot in price over the next 10 years.

If you have to sell it before 10 years, you might take a loss.

Coke's stock is certainly not risk-free.

It could certainly go down 20-50% in a bear market.

But it does pay you significantly more than Treasuries or savings accounts.

We can see this, because it has a higher yield.

Furthermore, Coke has been paying a quarterly dividend since 1920.

And it has increased its dividend every year for the past 55 years.

That makes it a more reliable institution than most governments.

Here's another cool thing about dividend yields.

Let's say that you bought some shares of Coke during the 2008 financial crisis.

During 2008, you could have bought as many shares as you wanted at $22/share.

Back then, the annual dividend was only $0.76 per share.

So if you bought the stock at 22, your dividend yield was $0.76 divided by 22, or 3.45%

Pretty close to where the dividend yield is now.

It's hard to get excited when you see a dividend yield of just 3.45%.

But look what happened next.

Today the annual dividend is $1.56.

That's a dividend yield of just 3.75%, if you buy Coke here at 41.55.

But if you were wise enough to pick up some shares of Coke at 22.00 during the 2008 crisis, the dividend yield on your investment is this:

$1.56 divided by 22, or 7.09%.

There's not a single super-safe investment around today that will pay you 7.09% a year.

Even better: this dividend yield will probably move up every year, as Coke continues to increase their dividend.

If you bought Coke in 2008, there's another way that you've made money.

The stock price has moved from 22.00 to 41.55.

If you bought a thousand shares of Coke, you've made $19,550 from the stock price moving (41.55 minus 22.00 times 1000)

You've also collected these dividend payments along the way:

- 2008: $760
- 2009: $820
- 2010: $880
- 2011: $940
- 2012: $1,020
- 2013: $1,120
- 2014: $1,220
- 2015: $1,320
- 2016: $1,400
- 2017: $1,480

These cash payments hit your account three times every year, whether you were sick or well, working at the office, or lounging on the beach.

Coke had its IPO back in 1919.

You could have bought a single share at the IPO for $40 (that's not the split-adjusted price).

If you reinvested the dividends that you received over the years, that Coke investment is now worth about $10,000,000.

There's a reason why many families in Atlanta still speak of The Coca-Cola Company in reverent, hushed tones.

Shares of Coke are passed from one generation to the next, and children are taught never to sell.

"Dividend reinvestment" is when you take your dividends and buy more of the same (or a different) dividend stock with them.

It's like using the cash from one little cash machine to buy some more little cash machines.

Imagine having some shares of stock that pay you a dividend.

Now imagine that those shares of stock were paid for completely using only the money from a dividend.

And that that dividend itself came from shares of stock that were bought with money from another dividend.

Infinite regress is hard on philosophers, but fun when you're dealing with dividend stocks.

So how can we find other great dividend-paying stocks like Coke?

The next chapter will teach you how.

3

A POWERFUL SHORTCUT FOR PICKING DIVIDEND STOCKS

When you're dealing with biological organisms like plants or people, the probability of dying rises with age.

An old man is more likely to die before a young man.

However, when you're dealing with non-organic structures, the probability of "dying" actually decreases with age.

Non-biological structures actually age in reverse.

For example, people having been reading and watching Shakespeare's plays for about 400 years.

Probabilistically speaking, they will continue to do so for another 400 years.

People have been listening to Beethoven for about 200 years.

Probabilistically speaking, they will continue to do so for another 200 years.

On the other hand, people have been listening to Taylor Swift for about 12 years.

We would expect her music to last only another 12 years.

However, if people listen to her music for another 5 years from today, we would expect her music to last for another 17 years from that point in time.

Again, we're talking about probabilities here.

Take a basket of old things, and it will last longer than a basket of newer things.

Chopsticks, the fork, and the chair were invented a long time ago.

They are elegant solutions that have withstood the test of time.

That's one reason that old things age in reverse.

The longer they've been around, the longer they will likely be around.

This is what's called "the Lindy Effect."

It takes its name from the Lindy Delicatessen in New York City, where actors used to gather and conduct postmortems on Broadway shows.

They began to notice that if a show had been around for 100 days, it was most likely to last another 100 days.

If it had been around for 2 years, it was most likely to last for another 2 years.

So what does this have to do with dividend stocks?

Well, it turns out that companies also age in reverse.

Wells Fargo has been around for about 166 years.

So we would expect it to last for another 166 years.

On the other hand, Facebook has been around for only 14 years.

Probabilistically speaking, we would expect it to be around for only another 14 years.

Of course it's impossible to know the life expectancy of a single company with any degree of certainty.

However, when dealing with baskets of companies, the Lindy Effect is a useful tool.

If we want to own dividend-paying stocks that will be around for a long time.
..

(Because it doesn't do us any good if a stock pays us a few dividends and then goes bankrupt, driving the stock price to zero)

Then we should probably look at dividend-paying stocks that have been around for a long time.

Companies that have managed to survive for a long time have probably survived because they are robust in some ways that may or may not be readily apparent.

Companies that have been paying a dividend every year for a very long time are likely to continue to do so.

Companies that have been increasing their dividend every year for a very long time are also likely to continue to do so.

There is a name for this group of elite stocks.

They could have called them "Lindy Stocks."

Instead they chose the name:

"Dividend Aristocrats."

These are all large companies that are part of the S&P 500 Index.

To be a part of this elite group, a company must have increased its dividend every year for the past 25 years.

As of today (27 May 2018), there are currently 53 Dividend Aristocrats:

3M CO (MMM)

A.O. SMITH (AOS)

ABBOTT LABORATORIES (ABT)

ABBVIE INC (ABBV)

AFLAC INC (AFL)

AIR PRODUCTS AND CHEMICALS (APD)

ARCHER DANIELS MIDLAND CO (ADM)

AT&T INC (T)

AUTOMATIC DATA PROCESSING (ADP)

BECTON DICKINSON AND CO (BDX)

BROWN-FORMAN CORP (BF.B)

CARDINAL HEALTH INC (CAH)

CHEVRON CORP (CVX)

CINCINNATI FINANCIAL CORP (CINF)

CINTAS CORP (CTAS)

CLOROX CO (CLX)

COCA-COLA CO/THE (KO)

COLGATE-PALMOLIVE CO (CL)

CONSOLIDATED EDISON INC (ED)

DOVER CORP (DOV)

ECOLAB INC (ECL)

EMERSON ELECTRIC CO (EMR)

EXXON MOBIL CORP (XOM)

FEDERAL REALTY INV. TRUST (FRT)

FRANKLIN RESOURCES INC (BEN)

GENERAL DYNAMICS (GD)

GENUINE PARTS CO (GPC)

HORMEL FOODS CORP (HRL)

ILLINOIS TOOL WORKS INC (ITW)

JOHNSON & JOHNSON (JNJ)

KIMBERLY-CLARK CORP (KMB)

LEGGETT & PLATT INC (LEG)

LOWE'S COS INC (LOW)

MCCORMICK & CO INC (MKC)

MCDONALD'S CORP (MCD)

MEDTRONIC INC (MDT)

NUCOR CORP (NUE)

PENTAIR PLC (PNR)

PEPSICO INC (PEP)

PPG INDUSTRIES INC (PPG)

PRAXAIR (PX)

PROCTER & GAMBLE CO (PG)

ROPER TECHNOLOGIES (ROP)

S&P GLOBAL (SPGI)

SHERWIN-WILLIAMS CO (SHW)

STANLEY BLACK & DECKER INC (SWK)

SYSCO CORP (SYY)

T. ROWE PRICE GROUP INC (TROW)

TARGET CORP (TGT)

VF CORP (VFC)

W W GRAINGER INC (GWW)

WAL-MART STORES INC (WMT)

WALGREENS BOOTS ALLIANCE (WBA)

You can get the latest list of Dividend Aristocrats here:

Many of these are household names.

Some are not.

But all of them have raised their dividends every year for the past 25 years.

These are the bluest of the blue chips.

So let's say that you have $1,000 to invest.

Take $1,000 and divide it by 53, to get about $18.86.

Go to your brokerage account and buy $18.86 of each of these 53 stocks.

If Coke is trading at 41.55, you will buy $18.86 divided by 41.55 equals 0.4539 shares (that's what's called a "fractional share," since you need $41.55 to buy one full share of Coke today).

Now buying 53 stocks can be a bit time-consuming.

Fortunately, there is a short cut.

You can just buy the ProShares S&P 500 Dividend Aristocrats ETF.

The ticker is NOBL, and this ETF (exchange-traded fund) trades just like a stock.

You can purchase it using any brokerage account.

Today NOBL trades at $62.65 per share.

So if you have $1,000, you can buy 15.96 shares of NOBL (1000 divided by 62.65).

You'll pay an expense ratio of 0.35% to own this ETF.

What this means is that if you invest $1,000 in this ETF, you will pay them $3.50 every year for the privilege of owning their ETF.

NOBL will collect all of the dividends paid by these Dividend Aristocrats and then pass them on to you every three months (quarterly).

You can read more about this ETF here:

http://www.proshares.com/dividend_growers/nobl.html

If you are just getting started, it might be wise to slowly "cost average" into NOBL.

How would you feel if you invested the full $1,000 today, and then tomorrow all stocks started going down for the next 12 months?

To avoid this, you can divided your $1,000 into 12 chunks of $83.33.

Invest $83.33 into NOBL every 15th day (or whatever day you choose) of the month for the next 12 months.

Doing so will get you invested into NOBL at around the average price that it will be trading at over the next year.

If it goes down next month, you'll be happy because you'll get to buy more of it at a cheaper price.

If it goes up next month, you'll also be happy because you already own some.

Cost-averaging into a stock or ETF is a great way to avoid "analysis paralysis."

So we can buy all 53 stocks in our brokerage account.

Or we can just buy an ETF like NOBL.

There's a third way, as well.

Reading through the list of stocks above, a lot of the names probably jumped out at you.

Names like:

Coke

Exxon Mobil

Hershey's

AT&T

Pepsico

Procter & Gamble

Johnson & Johnson

McDonald's

Colgate-Palmolive

Clorox

3M

Lowe's

Kimberly-Clark

Sherwin-Williams

Target

Walmart

Walgreens

That's 17 names.

These are companies make the products and services that we all use almost every day of our lives.

Instead of owning 53 stocks, you will probably be fine owning just these 17 Dividend Aristocrats.

Stock market theorists generally agree that you can get most of the benefits of diversification by holding only 15-20 stocks, as long as they are in different sectors.

(Diversification is simply keeping your eggs in lots of different baskets; that way, if one or two stocks crash, you still have 15 stocks that are plugging away and continuing to pay you dividends).

It's definitely easier to buy 17 stocks than it is to buy 53.

Feel free to adjust the above list to suit your own market intuitions.

Personally, I'm quite worried about Exxon's ability to replace its oil reserves.

You might be worried that Amazon is going to put Target and Walmart out of business in the next 5 years.

So feel free to pick 15-20 stocks from the list of Dividend Aristocrats that suit your own personal preferences.

The most important thing is not to overthink it.

As we discussed with NOBL, you may wish to cost average into these 15-20 stocks over 12 months.

Maybe just buy a 1/12 size position every month in each stock.

Whatever you decide to do, the most important thing is to just get started.

The sooner you start investing in dividend stocks, the sooner you will start building wealth.

I want to mention one last great resource for finding the best dividend stocks:

Warren Buffett.

Go to this link and click on his latest letter:

http://www.berkshirehathaway.com/letters/letters.html

Scroll down about halfway, and you will see a list of his latest stock holdings.

This is also a very good pool to fish in.

For example, three names jump out at me:

American Express (AXP)

Wells Fargo (WFC)

Apple (AAPL)

Buffett has owned American Express since 1964.

He has owned Wells Fargo since 1990.

Both financial companies ran into trouble during the 2008 financial crisis, but have recovered nicely—as have their dividends.

Apple is Buffett's first real tech stock pick.

It has not been around long enough to qualify as a Dividend Aristocrat.

Nevertheless, Apple's management is excellent, and they are doing a great job of returning profits to shareholders in the form of dividends.

The Apple ecosystem does a good job of locking in consumers.

And it's a world-class brand, like Coke.

Buffett certainly expects Apple to be around for a very long time, and to continue to increase its dividends over time.

The Lindy Effect is a much better stock-picker than most human beings.

That being said, I would also trust any of Buffett's stock picks as good long-term dividend holdings.

In the next chapter, we will discuss where to open up a brokerage account, so that you can buy your first dividend stock.

4

ROBINHOOD TO THE RESCUE

Dividend investing has recently become much easier for the little guy.

The average trading commission in the late 1980's was around $45.

Today, thanks to Robinhood, it's zero.

You read that correctly:

You will not be charged a commission (fee) to buy stocks with Robinhood.

Technically, you will still be charged a few pennies when you sell stocks using Robinhood, but that is a U.S. SEC fee.

If you sell $1 million of stock, you will only get charged $23.10.

So it's pretty much negligible.

Robinhood also allows you to buy fractional shares (i.e. less than 1 share), which is very helpful when you are first getting started and have a small account size.

Even better, there is no account minimum to open up an account.

You can literally open up an account with Robinhood and deposit just 10 cents.

To open up an account, you can go here on your laptop or phone:

I have no connection with Robinhood, other than I like and use their services.

Go to the website, or download the Robinhood app to your phone.

Fill out the required information.

You'll then be allowed to "fund" your Robinhood account by linking it to one of your online bank accounts, and telling them how much money to transfer over to Robinhood.

Once your account is funded, you'll be all ready to trade.

When you start trying to buy stocks on Robinhood, you'll quickly discover that there are 2 kinds of execution orders.

Market orders, and limit orders.

A market order tells Robinhood to get you into the stock as quickly as possible.

A "buy market order" tells them to buy the stock as quickly as possible, regardless of price

A "sell market order" tells them to sell the stock as quickly as possible, regardless of price.

Market orders usually work fine with Dividend Aristocrats, because these stocks are very liquid (they trade a lot of shares).

If you do a market order in the middle of the trading day for one of the Dividend Aristocrats, you'll probably be fine.

Stocks tend to wiggle around a lot more when the market first opens up in the morning—and when the market is about to close in the afternoon.

You definitely don't want to use a market order at these times.

To be safe, I would recommend that you use only limit orders when you are first getting started.

A "buy limit order" tells Robinhood to buy your stock at or below a certain price that you get to specify as part of the order (say, 41.55).

A buy limit order looks something like this:

Buy 10 shares of KO at 41.55 limit.

or

Buy 10 shares of KO at 41.55, or better.

When you are buying a stock, you are obviously happy to pay less per share.

The lower the price you pay, the higher your initial dividend yield will be.

A buy limit order helps you get this done.

It will be executed at the price that you specify, or lower.

If the stock doesn't trade at that price or lower, you may need to cancel the order, and put in a buy limit order at a slightly higher price.

If this happens, don't worry about it.

We fully expect KO to eventually trade above 100 or more, so it doesn't really matter whether we pay 41.55, or 41.70 for our shares.

If you are not able to watch the market during the day, enter your buy limit order at the same price that the stock closed at the previous day.

That way, your order can be executed while you are at work—provided that the stock trades at or below that price level.

Robinhood also provides a daily chart of every stock.

By looking at these charts, you can see the high prices and the low prices that the stock has traded at over the past week or past month.

That may give you a better idea of where to place your buy limit order.

Again, don't overthink it.

The point is to keep accumulating these stocks over time at many different price levels.

You can use fresh cash to buy these stocks.

Or you can use the cash that starts to build up in your Robinhood account from stocks that have paid you a dividend.

When you are first getting started, it's a good idea to add a certain amount of money to your brokerage account every single month.

This has been called "Paying Yourself First."

For some people, this might be $20.

For others, it might be $2,000.

Whatever the amount, just remember to always pay yourself first.

When you use your spare cash to buy more dividend stocks, rather than taking another cruise or buying a flat screen TV, you are investing in your own future.

The sooner you get started, and the more money you are able to contribute every month, the larger your nest egg will be at the end.

That's how Ronald Read got to $8 million, in spite of having only a janitor's salary.

At the present, Robinhood does not yet offer IRA's or other kinds of retirement accounts, but I believe that they will in the near future.

When you are buying dividend stocks in an IRA, you don't need to pay taxes on your dividend income that year.

Instead you will pay taxes on your compounded gains once you start to withdraw money from the IRA in your retirement.

One problem with investing in a taxable account (the only kind that Robinhood currently offers) is that you will need to pay taxes on your dividend income every year.

Every year in January or February, Robinhood will send you a document called a "1099."

They will also send a copy to the IRS.

This 1099 will tell you how much dividend income you collected in the previous year, so that you can calculate your taxes on it.

If your income levels are low enough (below $77,201 for a married couple filing jointly), you will probably not owe any taxes on your dividend income.

If your income is higher, you may owe up to 23.80%.

Again, be sure to consult with a tax professional (which I am not).

If you are short on cash, you may wish to leave 15% to 23.80% of your dividend income in your Robinhood account, and not reinvest it in dividend stocks.

That way, you will have the cash available to pay your dividend taxes the following year at tax time.

5

WHEN TO SELL A STOCK

There's another kind of limit order that I did not touch on in the previous chapter.

A "sell limit order" lets you sell a stock at a specified price or higher.

A sell limit order looks like this:

Sell 10 shares of KO at 50.00 limit

or

Sell 10 shares of KO at 50.00 or better

If the stock trades at or above that price and there is a buyer who wants at least 10 shares of KO, your order will be "filled," and your shares of Coke will be sold.

There's a reason that I did not dwell on sell orders in the previous chapter.

In my opinion, you will almost never need to sell your shares of Dividend Aristocrats.

As Warren Buffett is fond of saying:

"The best time to sell a stock is. . . never."

Elsewhere, Buffett qualifies this statement, by emphasizing that he is only referring to wonderful businesses run by wonderful managements.

Some financial advisors will tell you to sell off some shares of a stock if it has become too large a part of your portfolio.

I think this is a big mistake.

As Buffett quips:

> "To suggest that an investor should sell off portions of his most successful investments simply because they have come to dominate his portfolio is akin to suggesting that the Bulls trade Michael Jordan because he has become so important to the team."

It's definitely a big mistake to sell your winners.

It's also a mistake to sell your Dividend Aristocrats just because they have gone down in price.

During a nasty bear market, some of them may go down as much as 50%.

Please don't sell.

Turn off your computer and don't even look at where they are trading.

Even better, add some fresh cash to your account, and buy more of them when they are down.

If you buy a stock when it is down 50% from its high, and it returns to its old high, you will have made not 50%, but 100% on your money.

That is too good of a return to turn down.

If you see some scary news about one of your stocks, ignore it.

If the CEO gets fired, ignore it.

There's only one situation where I think you should sell a Dividend Aristocrat.

If they cut the dividend, sell it the next day.

Some stocks that cut their dividend are able to have a comeback.

But most are not.

If a Dividend Aristocrat cannot pay its dividend, it means one of 2 things:

1. The management is no longer very shareholder-friendly-- in which case you want out.
2. The business has deteriorated to the point that it is no longer able to pay the dividend that it once was—in which case you want out.

To get out, use a sell limit order that is set at the previous day's low price.

A fallen Dividend Aristocrat is a sorry sight to behold.

Think, Eastman Kodak.

Kodak paid a dividend every year since 1902.

Then, devastated by digital cameras, it slashed its dividend by 72% in 2003.

By 2012, the stock was almost worthless and the company filed for bankruptcy protection.

Be ruthless with your Dividend Aristocrats.

If they cut the dividend, kick them out of the castle immediately.

While we're on the topic of fallen dividend stocks, there's one more thing to tell you.

If you ever see an ordinary stock (not a REIT or MLP) with a very high dividend yield (6% or higher), it's almost always a sign that something is wrong with the company.

Occasionally, you will see yields like this during an especially nasty bear market, when everyone is dumping their stocks indiscriminately

But if you see it during a normal market, something is very very wrong.

Stocks tend to move down right before a dividend cut or omission.

This gives them the illusion of having a high dividend yield.

However, the high dividend yield is not real.

Once the dividend is cut, the dividend yield will trade in a more normal range.

You will never be paid that illusory high yield, and you will probably get caught in a stock that continues to go down.

Don't make the mistake of chasing high-yielding stocks—it's a mug's game.

6

HOW TO SURVIVE (AND EVEN PROFIT FROM) A BEAR MARKET

I f you spend enough time in the markets, there is a 100% chance that you will experience a bear market in your lifetime.

And probably multiple bear markets.

If you've lived through one, you know how difficult they can be.

Bear markets usually last 6 months to 2.5 years.

As we've mentioned, some of your Dividend Aristocrats may go down as much as 50% in a bear market.

There will be some mornings when you check your stocks' prices and will not believe what you see.

Some of them may be down 5-10% on the day.

You'll rub your eyes, and not believe what you are seeing.

You'll think you're having a bad dream.

When this happens, I want you to buy more Dividend Aristocrats.

I don't care if jets have just crashed into a skyscraper, or we're at war, or banks are blowing up around the country.

If you have the cash, please buy more.

There are a number of reasons that this is a good idea.

First, many people and institutions sell stocks during a bear market even though they don't want to.

When I was running a hedge fund during the last financial crisis, I had to sell some stocks in order to give one of my investors his money back.

I knew that these stocks were massively undervalued.

But I was still forced to sell them.

When I was done selling these shares for my hedge fund, I immediately started buying them in my personal accounts.

One of these stocks is now up 7x from where my fund was forced to sell it.

So don't assume that it is the smart money that is selling during a bear market.

It is usually just people and institutions that have gotten margin calls or redemption requests.

It is mostly forced selling.

And Mom and Pop investors who are panicking for no reason.

I don't want you to be one of them.

Most of the time, you should not even be checking on stock prices.

And especially not during a bear market.

Here's a rule for you to follow:

Never login to your Robinhood account, or check stock prices online, unless you have cash and are ready to buy some more Dividend Aristocrats.

If you follow this rule, you will save yourself an enormous amount of psychological distress.

When one of your stocks is down 50% from where you bought it, I want you to buy more, if you are financially able.

When it recovers to its previous highs, you will have made 100% on your money, as we discussed before.

Are you the kind of person who gets excited when you see a new car marked down 20%?

Or a furniture sale, where every item is 50% off?

If so, you'll love a bear market.

It's an opportunity to accumulate wonderful companies at markdown prices.

As Warren Buffett is famous for saying:

> "Be fearful when others are greedy, and greedy when others are fearful."

A bear market is a great time to take all of that dividend cash that has been piling up in your Robinhood account and reinvest it in the same Dividend Aristocrats that paid you the dividends.

That's exactly what Warren Buffett does during a bear market.

When a stock is down a lot, that dividend cash will buy you many more shares than it normally would.

You'll now own a greater percentage of a fantastic company than you did before.

Bear markets are how the rich get richer.

It's a Darwinian purge that wipes out the weak hands.

If you don't really know why you own a stock, there is a good chance that you will be tempted to dump it during a bear market.

That's why I want you to read this book a couple of times.

It's a short book, but packed with knowledge.

I want you to make this knowledge your own.

You have to feel it in your bones, if you are to be successful.

There is another reason that bear markets are good for Dividend Aristocrats.

During a stock market crash and economic downturn, smaller competitors will often be forced out of business.

If you are a Mom and Pop home improvement store, there's a very good chance that you didn't make it through the last downturn.

There's a good chance that you had to shut your doors.

Now your old customers go to Home Depot or Lowe's.

As a result, those 2 companies now have greater market share, and their stocks are worth more.

A bear market is also a perfect time for a Dividend Aristocrat to buy out one of its ailing rivals.

Exxon Mobil is famous for buying its rivals' assets for pennies on the dollar during market wipe-outs.

So, during a bear market, not only do you get to buy a wonderful business at a markdown price.

But that wonderful business is probably actively increasing its intrinsic value by increasing its market share during the downturn.

It's a double blessing for the savvy investor in Dividend Aristocrats.

That's why, in a bear market, you should only be buying shares, not selling.

7

DIVIDEND CAPTURE STRATEGIES

G o to Google and type in:

"KO ex dividend date"

If you do that today, you'll come up with a few websites that will tell you that Coke next goes "ex-dividend" on 6/14/2018.

What that means is this:

If you own the stock on 13 June 2018, you will get paid a dividend of $0.39 on 2 July 2018.

But if you buy the stock on 14 June 2018 or later, you will not be entitled to that quarterly dividend payment.

The ex-dividend date of a stock represents the cut-off point for receiving the dividend.

This has led many to make the following observation:

I only need to own Coke for one day to collect that dividend payment.

So I'm going to buy the stock on 6/13/2018, and then try to sell it the next day for approximately the same price that I paid for it.

I'm going to get paid a $0.39 dividend, so even if the stock itself falls $0.39,

I'll still break-even.

Right now, KO is trading for 42.00, so I'll make 0.39 divided by 42 or 0.92% on my money.

That's more than some savings accounts pay in a whole year.

Now what if I did this across 20 different Dividend Aristocrats?

Most of them pay quarterly dividends, so that's 80 different opportunities throughout the year to capture dividends.

Now in theory, this strategy should not work.

This is because a stock should fall on the ex-dividend date by exactly the amount of the quarterly dividend to be paid.

Imagine that you sent a big check to your friends four times a year.

On the day that the checks were cashed, one would expect the value of your net worth to fall by that exact amount.

But stocks are different.

Because they wiggle around, it is quite possible to buy a stock the day before it goes ex-dividend, and then sell it at the same price on the ex-dividend date.

It doesn't work all of the time, but it does work a lot more often than it should.

If you are patient, and use limit orders for your buying and selling, it is very possible to make this strategy work for you.

That being said, I personally don't do it anymore.

I like to hold my Dividend Aristocrats in a separate account.

That's where I buy them, and hopefully never need to sell them.

I've personally found dividend capture strategies to be more work than they're worth.

If I want to day trade, or swing trade, I'll pick more volatile stocks.

I discuss these trading strategies in my other Kindle books.

One of the nicest things about the Dividend Aristocrats strategy is that it is so low maintenance.

I work hard in my other trading accounts, so it is nice to have one investing account where I can buy dividend stocks and park them for the long-term.

It's a "set it and forget it" strategy.

I like to let dividend reinvestment and compounding do the heavy lifting for me in this account.

There's one other problem with the dividend capture strategy.

You'll end up paying higher taxes.

As we mentioned before, you can pay 0% on your dividend income in the U.S. for 2018, for taxable income up to $38,600 for single filers and up to $77,200 for joint filers.

I should now specify that this only works for what are called "qualified dividends."

Most dividends from U.S. companies are "qualified"— but only if you own the stock for more than 60 days during the 121-day period that begins 60-days before the ex-dividend date.

Yes, that's a mess to figure out.

It's another reason why it's just easier to buy and hold dividend companies for the long-term.

That way, you dividends will always be "qualified" and will be eligible for favorable tax treatment.

If you are going to do a dividend capture strategy, try to do it in an IRA or other tax-deferred accounts, so that you can side-step this tax mess.

If you must do it in a regular taxable account, just keep in mind that you will be paying higher taxes on your dividend income, if the dividends are not "qualified."

That's OK, as long as your after-tax return is high enough to justify the extra work.

That's a judgment call that every investor will need to make for himself or herself.

8

HOW NOT TO OVERPAY FOR DIVIDEND STOCKS

I f you pay too much, even the best company can turn out to be a bad investment.

This is because the stock market is, for the most part, an excellent discounting mechanism.

It takes into account all current information and future growth prospects and tries to bake them into the current stock price.

In early 2000, Microsoft was trading at around $57 per share.

At that time, it was trading at a P/E (price to earnings ratio) of roughly 57.

The market average P/E is somewhere around 15.

So clearly, Microsoft was expensive in 2000, as measured by its P/E ratio

You were paying $57 for each $1 of current earnings.

For the average stock at the average time, you'd only have to pay $15 for $1 of earnings.

Microsoft clearly had a rosy future in 2000.

It was in the top 5 tech companies at the time.

And it's still one of the top 5 tech companies in 2018.

However, if you bought shares of Microsoft at such a high P/E in 2000, you did not do well on your investment.

Ten years later, in 2010, Microsoft was still trading 50% down from its 2000 highs.

In fact, Microsoft did not trade at new highs until late 2016.

16 years is a long time to go without any capital gains.

And while you were waiting, you did not get paid much of a dividend.

The moral of this story?

Even the best Dividend Aristocrat, if priced too high, is not a good investment.

The only problem is that it is harder than you would think to tell when a stock is overpriced.

In 2000, Microsoft was overvalued, but some other stocks were not.

I have three possible solutions.

First solution:

As we discussed, just cost-average into every position. If you buy a 1/12 position in a dividend stock every month for 12 months (or 1/24 over 24 months), you should end up with a decent average price.

At least you won't be buying all of your shares at the exact highs.

This is the agnostic solution to price.

Second solution:

Create a ladder.

So if I had $10,000 to invest in KO, I would buy $1,000 of stock at its current price of 42.00.

Then another $1,000 if it trades down to 41.00.

Then another $1,000 if it trades down to 40.00, etc.

The only problem with this strategy?

If KO stays around 42.00 for the next 5 years, I'll only have a 1/10 position on.

I'll be under-invested in KO, and missing out on all of those nice dividends for 5 years.

This ladder strategy makes the most sense in the late years of a bull market.

As I write this on 27 May 2018, the bull market has been raging for the past 9 years.

We're overdue for a bear market.

So now would not be a good time to allocate my whole chunk of change to stocks.

Cost-averaging, or a ladder might make the most sense.

Third solution:

If the stock that you are considering is a Dividend Aristocrat and it has a dividend yield between 2.50% and 4.50% today, it is probably reasonably fairly priced (in the current interest rate environment).

If the dividend yield is below 2.50%, the stock is probably over-priced, and you should wait to purchase it.

If the dividend yield is over 4.50%, there is probably something wrong.

Either the company has an enormous amount of debt or underfunded pension obligations (like AT&T), which makes the stock more risky.

Or the market is pricing in the chance of a dividend cut.

Either way, you are better off sticking with the 2.50% to 4.50% dividend yield range.

That's where the more normal healthy companies will be found.

9

THE EASIEST PATH TO WEALTH

The greatest advantage that you can have in the stock market is not knowledge.

And it's not insider information.

The greatest advantage that you can have in the stock market is simply:

Time.

Albert Einstein once called compounding the "eighth wonder of the world."

If you combine compounding with time, you have the perfect recipe for building wealth.

Let me give you an example.

In 1988 and 1989, Warren Buffett bought shares of Coke at a split-adjusted average price of just $2.45

Today Coke trades at around $42.00 per share.

What is more remarkable is that Coke will pay $1.56 per share in dividends in 2018.

That is a dividend yield of 63% on Buffett's original purchase price.

Given enough time, any of us can achieve a dividend yield like this.

This is why it is so important to get started investing in dividend stocks when you are young.

It's a ridiculously simple way to build extreme wealth.

And it's a path that's open to anyone with some foresight and a little discipline.

If there is a child or teenager in your life, please pass along a copy of this book to them.

Or email me their address at matt@trader.university and I will send them a free paperback copy of this book.

Or better yet, you should buy them a few shares of Coke, McDonald's, and Johnson & Johnson and hide them away for them.

If you can, give your kids stocks instead of toys.

Instead of taking them to McDonald's, set up a custodial account and sock away a few shares of McDonald's for them.

Instead of buying them an iPad, take the money and buy some Apple stock for the long run.

You'll be glad that you did.

In the meantime, I'm happy to help you along on your own investing journey

If you have any questions about dividend stocks, or just want to say hi, write to me at matt@trader.university

I love to hear from my readers, and I try to answer every email personally.

I am currently getting a huge volume of email, so please keep bugging me if you don't hear back right away.

I would like to connect personally with each of you, and see if I can help you in any way.

Thanks for purchasing this book and reading it all the way to the end.

If you enjoyed this book and found it useful, I'd be very grateful if you'd post an honest review on Amazon.

All that you need to do is to **click here** (or go to www.trader-books.com) and then click on the correct book cover.

Then click the blue link next to the yellow stars that says "customer reviews."

You'll then see a gray button that says "Write a customer review"—click that and you're good to go.

If you would like to learn more ways to make money in the markets, check out my other Kindle books on the next page.

ABOUT THE AUTHOR

Hi there!

My name is Matthew Kratter.

I am the founder of Trader University, and the best-selling author of multiple books on trading and investing.

I have more than 20 years of trading experience, including working at multiple hedge funds.

Most individual traders and investors are at a huge disadvantage when it comes to the markets.

Most are unable to invest in hedge funds.

Yet, when they trade their own money, they are competing against computer algorithms, math PhD's, and multi-billion dollar hedge funds.

I've been on the inside of many hedge funds.

I know how professional traders and investors think and approach the markets.

And I am committed to sharing their trading strategies with you in my books and courses.

When I am not trading or writing new books, I enjoy skiing, hiking, and otherwise hanging out in the Rocky Mountains with my wife, kids, and dogs.

If you enjoyed this book, you may also enjoy my other Kindle titles, which are available here:

http://www.trader.university

Just click on the tab that says "Books."

Or send me an email at matt@trader.university.

I would love to hear from you.

DISCLAIMER

While the author has used his best efforts in preparing this book, he makes no representations or warranties with respect to the accuracy or completeness of the contents of this book and specifically disclaims any implied warranties or merchantability or fitness for a particular purpose. The advice and strategies contained herein may not be suitable for your situation.

You should consult with a legal, financial, tax, or other professional where appropriate. Neither the publisher nor the author shall be liable for any loss of profit or any other commercial damages, including but not limited to special, incidental, consequential, or other damages.

This book is for educational purposes only. The views expressed are those of the author alone, and should not be taken as expert instruction or commands. The reader is responsible for his or her own actions.

Adherence to all applicable laws and regulations, including international, federal, state, and local laws, is the sole responsibility of the purchaser or reader.

Neither the author nor the publisher assumes any responsibility or liability whatsoever on the behalf of the purchaser or reader of these materials.

Any perceived slight of any individual or organization is purely unintentional.

Past performance is not necessarily indicative of future performance.